The Gingerbread Micro-man

Danny Waddell
Illustrated by Jon Stuart

OXFORD

In this story

Max

Tiger

Mum

a bird

Mum was making gingerbread men.

Max and Tiger were playing.
Then Tiger lost the football.

Mum went next door to get more raisins. Tiger had a plan.

Max and Tiger went inside.
They pushed the buttons ...

They played football.

Then Mum came back!
Max and Tiger hid.

Tiger played a trick on Mum.

Mum took the tray. She did not see Tiger.

Tiger jumped off the tray.
Then he ran outside.

A bird saw Tiger.

You can't catch me!

Max came just in time.

Run, run as fast as you can!

13

They pushed the buttons ...

Then they went back inside.

"Here you go," said Mum.
"No, thank you!" said Tiger.

How to make gingerbread men

Mix

Roll

Cut

Decorate

Bake

Eat (before they run away)!

Sam got a pip. 'Put it in the bin, Sam.'
But Sam did not.

Sam put on a hat and a mac.
Sam got a pan.

Sam pops the pip in the pan.
Sam puts a bag on top.

Sam got a pot.

Sam pops the pip in the pot.

Sam taps the top of the pot.

Sam put a tag on the pot.
Sam got the tin can.

It is hot.

Sam got the pot.

Sam's pip!